Always, Sometimes, Never

by Ellen Cynthia Low

illustrated by Emily Arnold McCully

My name is Alice.

But I always like to be called Allie.

I always go to sleep with my animals.

Sometimes I make breakfast in the morning.

I always pick out my own clothes.

Sometimes I forget to match the socks.

But there is one thing I never, ever do.

I never, ever pet that big cat!

At school, I always draw funny people.

Sometimes they do not have noses.

My teacher always hangs up our work.

Sometimes I write my name in BIG letters.

After school, I always jump off the bus.

But I never, ever pet that big cat!

I always play outside after my snack.

Sometimes I pretend I'm a superhero.

Even though I'm a superhero,

I never, ever pet that big cat!

Now I hear a funny sound. *Purr!*

I look down and see that cat!

I never, ever thought I would pet that cat.

But today I did!

And now I think I always, always will.